D0829239

Boys Don't Dance!

Story by
Rowena Cory Lindquist

Illustrations by
Tom Jellett

Rigby PM Plus Chapter Books
part of the Rigby PM Program
Emerald Level

Published by Harcourt Achieve Inc.
10801 N.MoPac Expressway
Building #3
Austin, TX 78759
www.harcourtachieve.com

Text © 2003 Thomson Learning Australia
Illustrations © 2003 Thomson Learning Australia
Originally published in Australia by Thomson Learning Australia

All rights reserved. No part of this publication may be
reproduced or transmitted in any form or by any means,
electronic or mechanical, including photocopying, recording,
taping, or any information storage and retrieval system,
without permission in writing from the publisher.

10 9 8 7 6 5 4
07 06

Boys Don't Dance!
    ISBN 0 7578 4125 2

Printed in China by 1010 Printing International Limited

Contents

Chapter 1   No Way Out   4

Chapter 2   Natural Rhythm   8

Chapter 3   Adrian Parker   16

Chapter 4   Boys **Can** Dance!   18

Chapter 5   My Worst Nightmare   23

Chapter 6   Dancing on the Ceiling?   26

Chapter 7   Gotta Dance!   28

Chapter 1
No Way Out

"But Mom ..." I groaned. "Please don't make me do it."

Mom sighed. "Now, Luke. We've been through this before. You know I have to stay home with Brandon. You'll just have to do it."

There was no escape! I would have to take my little sister, Jessica, to her new dance class. Dancing! I hated dancing!

I gave it one last try. "You've got no idea what everyone at school will say if they find out!"

That was a **really** bad move. As if Mom would care what other people thought! "If you don't take Jessica to her dance class, she won't be able to go at all!" she said, with a disappointed look on her face. "Is that what you want?"

What could I say? Jessica can be annoying, but I didn't want her to miss out on her first class.

"Jessica!" I yelled. "Get your stuff together."

"I'm ready!" sang Jessica. "Let's go!"

As I opened the front door, Brandon, my little brother, came riding into the hall on his tricycle. "I wanna go too!" he said.

"You don't want to go, Brandon!" I told him. "Boys don't dance."

"Why not?"

"Because it's just for girls!"

Mom laughed. "Don't be silly, Luke," she said. "Some of the best dancers in the world are men!"

Yeah, right! I thought.

"Come on," said Jessica, as she pulled me through the front door. "I don't want to be late!"

Chapter 2
Natural Rhythm

The dance school had big glass doors. We could see the people dancing inside. I walked Jessica toward the classroom.

A lady, who must have been the teacher, came over to me. "Are you joining our dance class?" she asked.

My mouth dropped open. What a horrible thought!

"No!" I said. "My sister's joining."

"You'd better hurry then," said the teacher. "The class is about to start!" She clapped her hands and called for the class to begin. It was time for me to make my escape!

But Jessica grabbed my hand. "I'm scared," she said. "What if I can't do it?"

"Don't worry, Jess," I said. "You're a good dancer."

Her frightened eyes met mine. "Please stay."

Oh no! I thought. *That's all I need!* But what could I say? "All right, I'll stay!"

I watched as the dancers did some stretching exercises to warm up their muscles. We do stuff like that at soccer. It helps to prevent injuries.

Jessica glanced over her shoulder at me. I waved to her, then found a chair in the corner where I could stay out of sight. If anyone from school saw me here, I'd never hear the end of it!

The teacher switched on a CD player. Music boomed through the room. I sat up. *Hey*, I thought. *That music isn't bad!*

The dancers mimed taking sunglasses out of their pockets. I had to grin – they looked so cool! Then they had to click their fingers, tap their feet, skip sideways, spin, then do it all again in reverse. The steps didn't look so hard on their own, but when they were put together the dance was pretty complicated.

Jessica was trying, but she kept getting mixed up. The other dancers had been to more lessons, so they knew what to do. Poor Jess! I could see her face crumpling as she tried not to cry. The teacher noticed too. She asked Jessica if she wanted to have a rest.

Jess ran to the back of the classroom, and sat down. She looked so sad! I crept over to her. "Hey, Jess?"

She brushed at her face quickly. I pretended I hadn't seen the tears.

"Watch this." I walked her through the steps. "Click click, tap tap, skip sideways, spin around. Now, back the other way."

Hey, I thought as I danced. *This is kind of fun!* But I never would have admitted that to anyone else, of course!

After practicing the steps three or four times, Jess got the hang of it. She beamed at me, then ran to join the other dancers. I went back to my seat feeling pleased, and watched Jessica dancing happily. Before I knew it, the lesson was over.

Jessica ran over to me. "Did you see? Did you see? I did it!"

I nodded and smiled.

Just then, a group of girls my age rushed into the room. I groaned. Some of them were in my class at school! They looked my way and giggled. *I've got to get out of here now!* I thought. I tried to look cool as I headed for the door.

"Excuse me ..."

I jumped. It was the dancing teacher again. "I saw the way you helped your sister," she said with a smile. "You've got natural rhythm. Would you like to join our class? We need some more boys to dance in our concert."

How could I answer without being rude? "Uh ... I don't think so," I grunted. I grabbed Jessica. "Come on. Mom will be waiting."

Chapter 3
Adrian Parker

As I dragged my sister away from the dance school, she went on and on about dancing and how I should join the class. All of a sudden, I heard someone call my name. "Hey, Luke? Where have you been – ballet lessons?"

I spun around and saw Adrian Parker from school, with some of his crowd. My heart sank. Of all the people to see me coming out of a dance school, it had to be Adrian, the biggest bully in my class!

I tried to explain. "I was just taking my little sister to her dance class."

"Sure you were, Twinkle Toes!" sneered Adrian.

"Lay off, Adrian," I said. "You're just lucky that you don't have to take your sister to dance classes."

Adrian smirked. He did a little spin on his tippy-toes and fluttered his arms like fairy wings. The other guys laughed.

I'd had enough. I stormed off down the street. Jessica almost had to run to keep up with me.

Adrian shouted after me, "Can I borrow your tutu, Luke?" The other guys laughed again.

How was I ever going to live this down?

Chapter Four

Boys Can Dance!

When we got home, Jessica told Mom all about the class. "It was great, Mom! We're doing a concert, and I'm going to be in it! And guess what!" Her eyes went wide. "They asked Luke to join! They said he has **natural ribbon**."

Mom looked confused.

"Rhythm," I explained.

That night, Mom and Jessica watched a dance movie. I wasn't really interested, but I watched it anyway. *This is probably going to be a girl's movie*, I thought.

But I was wrong! Most of the dancers in the movie were men! I couldn't believe it.

"See?" said Mom. "I told you. Lots of men dance."

As I watched the movie, the music made my heart beat faster. I could hardly stop myself from getting up to dance!

Later that night, when Jessica had gone to bed, I put the movie on again. I pushed the coffee table out of the way, and fast-forwarded the video to the part where the guys did their big dance number. I copied the steps, and practiced them over and over again.

It was amazing! I'd never realized that dancing could be so much fun.

I was standing on the couch, waving my arms in the air, when Mom came into the room.

"Luke!" she gasped. "Why are you standing on the couch?"

I jumped down. Mom didn't look very happy, but I was too excited to be worried.

"Mom, watch this!" I rewound the video to the beginning of the dance.

The music came up from the ends of my toes and out through my fingertips. I didn't have to think about the steps – they just flowed.

When I'd finished, Mom clapped and clapped. "I never realized you were so talented!" she said. "Maybe you should think about taking dancing lessons."

I wasn't so sure. "But what if someone saw me?" I said. "Adrian Parker laughed at me just because I went into a dance school. What would he say if he saw me dancing?"

Mom laughed. "What's so important about Adrian Parker?" she asked. "Why should you care what he thinks?"

That just shows how much Mom knows. Imagine not worrying about Adrian Parker!

Chapter 5

My Worst Nightmare

When I got home from school the next day, I put on Jess's video again. No one else was home, so I pushed the coffee table against the wall, and danced along with the guys on the screen. Before long, I was making up extra steps, dancing around and around the living room.

I was getting right into it when Jessica walked into the room. "What are you doing?" she cried.

I stopped mid-step. "Um … dancing …"

Then I noticed that Jessica wasn't alone. There was another girl standing in the doorway.

"This is Tiffany Parker, from school," said Jessica. "She came over to see my dance costume."

Tiffany **Parker**? Adrian's sister? It was my worst nightmare!

"Come on," said Jessica to Tiffany. "Big brothers are so boring!"

Tiffany smirked. "At least **my** brother's not into dancing!"

I could have sunk through the floor. Tiffany was sure to tell Adrian that she'd seen me dancing. How was I going to get through school tomorrow?

Chapter 6

Dancing on the Ceiling?

Lucky for me, I got sick. I had to stay home from school! Mom went to the video store and brought home some movies for me to watch. Some of the movies were about dancing. One of them even had a man who danced right up the wall and over the ceiling!

Even some of the movies that weren't about dancing had scenes that looked like dancing. There was one with a fight scene that almost looked like ballet – but without the tights!

I thought about all the different ways people dance. Some people do ballet, some do ballroom dancing. There's even a group of people who do line dancing in the evenings in the school gym! People dance for all kinds of reasons. They dance in movies, and in TV ads. They dance because they're happy, and because they want to cheer themselves up. Some people even do traditional dances that have been done in their cultures for centuries.

Yeah. But they don't have to worry about Adrian!

Chapter 7

Gotta Dance!

A few days later, when I was feeling better, Mom asked me to take Jessica to her dance class again. "Here's the money for Jess's lesson," she said as we were leaving the house. "And here's extra money for you, just in case you decide to take the class too."

I didn't know what to say. I liked dancing, but I wasn't sure about taking lessons.

"You shouldn't worry so much about what the other kids might think," said Mom. It was as if she'd read my mind! "If you want to dance, go ahead!"

As we walked toward the dance school, I thought about all the guys in those movies. **They** hadn't worried about people laughing at them.

When we reached the school, I still wasn't sure what I should do.

"Are you going to join the class?" asked Jess.

My heart gave a funny little jump. All I had to do was say I'd try one class …

All of a sudden, I heard someone shout. "Hey, Twinkle Toes!"

I nearly jumped out of my skin! I turned around. Adrian and Tiffany were standing right behind me!

"What are you doing here?" I stammered.

"I had to take Tiffany to her new dance class," groaned Adrian. "What about you? Are you gonna dance too? Tiffany told me all about your living-room performance!" He laughed, convinced that he'd said something hilarious.

That did it! I decided that I wasn't going to worry about Adrian any more. I wanted to dance, and no one was going to stop me!

I took a deep breath. "Yes, Adrian," I said. "I **am** going to dance!"

And I walked into the dance class, with my head held high.